THE HOUSE ON THE LAKE

AIDAN FENNESSY

CURRENCY PRESS
SYDNEY

GRIFFIN
THEATRE
COMPANY

CURRENT THEATRE SERIES

First published in 2015
by Currency Press Pty Ltd,
PO Box 2287, Strawberry Hills, NSW, 2012, Australia
enquiries@currency.com.au
www.currency.com.au

in association with Griffin Theatre Company

Copyright: © Aidan Fennessy, 2015.

Cataloguing-in-publication data for this title is available from the National
Library of Australia website: www.nla.gov.au

Typeset by Dean Nottle for Currency Press.
Front cover shows Huw Higginson.
Cover photo by Brett Boardman.
Cover design by RE:

Currency Press acknowledges the Traditional Owners of the Country on which
we live and work. We pay our respects to all Aboriginal and Torres Strait
Islander Elders, past and present.

Contents

The House on the Lake was first performed by Black Swan State Theatre Company at Studio Centre, State Theatre Centre of WA, on 6 June 2014, with the following cast:

DAVID RAIL	Kenneth Ransom
DR ALICE LOWE	Marthe Rovik

Director, Stuart Halusz
Set & Costume Designer, India Mehta
Lighting Designer, Trent Suidgeest
Sound Designer / Composer, Brett Smith

CHARACTERS

ALICE LOWE, approximately 35 years of age

DAVID RAIL, approximately 50 years of age

SETTING

A room sparsely furnished with a bed, a table and two chairs. There are two high windows with security grilles above the bed. To the side is a door that leads to a bathroom. The entrance door is opposite. There is no internal handle on the door. It has a buzzer and an intercom next to it. There is no television, mirror or radio in the room. It has a comfortable but impersonal look about it. High up on the rear wall a CCTV camera looks down into the room.

SCRIPT NOTES

A dash at the start of a line indicates a held thought.

A dash at the end of a line indicates a cut-off.

A forward slash indicates overlapping dialogue.

This play went to press before the end of rehearsals and may differ from the play as performed.

SCENE ONE

DAVID *is sitting on the bed, wearing crisp hospital pyjamas.* ALICE *stands with some distance between herself and* DAVID. *In front of her on the table sits a file, a laptop, and various other documents. She is neatly and conservatively dressed with a white doctor's coat and a name tag. From outside we can hear the distant sound of rain. A cold early evening light streams in through the high windows. Occasionally throughout the play we hear the distant muffled sound of the hospital P.A. system. It's October twenty-second.* DAVID *looks at his pyjamas, looks around the room. He seems both alert and disorientated. He looks to the high windows and listens to the rain.*

ALICE: David…?

>   *Pause.*

DAVID: Yes?

>   *Pause.*

ALICE: Do you mind if I sit?

>   DAVID *gestures for her to take a seat.*

Thank you. My name is Alice. I'm here to help.

>   *She sits and opens her laptop then taps a few keys on the computer.*

DAVID: … You're a doctor?

ALICE: Yes.

>   *Pause.*

DAVID: Where am I?

ALICE: You're in a hospital…

DAVID: Why?

ALICE: … We're not sure.

>   DAVID *nods.*

You're okay, David. You're safe here.

DAVID: … Safe?

ALICE: Yes.

>   *Pause.*

DAVID: Where are my clothes?

ALICE: Everything's being looked after, David.

Pause.

DAVID: So… what's happened?

ALICE: We don't know yet… We're hoping you can help us find out…

DAVID: … We?

ALICE: What's the last thing you remember?

DAVID *thinks.*

DAVID: I woke up… here. In this room…

ALICE: Before that?

DAVID: … I was working in my office.

ALICE: What were you doing in your office?

DAVID: … Working…

Pause. DAVID *looks around the room. He shrugs and shakes his head.*

ALICE: That's okay… You're okay… We need to conduct a series of tests… David? You understand? To see where you're at. I thought we might just start with names and see how we go from there. So… my name is…?

DAVID *stares at her.*

Alice… and you are?

DAVID: David… David Rail.

ALICE: Good, David. So let's have a think about how we might go about remembering our names, yes? One way that we might use to remember a name is to use what is called—

DAVID: Remembering our names…

ALICE: Yes.

DAVID: I don't understand… why?

ALICE: This is just a simple—

DAVID: Have I met you before? [*Pause.*] Because you seem familiar. You seem familiar to me…

ALICE: Do you feel as if we have met before?

DAVID: … Have we?

ALICE: … Perhaps I have one of those faces.

DAVID: —

ALICE: Let's just concentrate on names. If you were to try and remember my name what kind of things do you think might help us out, David?

DAVID: What do I think might help *us* out…?

ALICE: Yes, David.

DAVID: One thing, Alice, do you mind?

ALICE: Not at all.

DAVID: Do you mind before *we* proceed? One thing…

ALICE: Yes, David.

DAVID: One thing before we go on… I appreciate you are simply trying to do your job and that in the course of executing that task you may have to interact with a whole range… a whole spectrum of… types… but can I ask you, Alice, and it's a little irksome so I'll try to phrase this as delicately as I can… but could you, Alice, could you possibly stop talking at me as if I were a vegetable?

> *Pause.*

ALICE: Of course.

DAVID: I respect that you're here in a professional capacity but it is a thing I've noted in regards to health professionals is that there is a tendency to 'talk down'… I am very happy for you to assert your authority within your given field, you understand, but you are confusing it, Alice, with broader assumptions. So do you mind? Can we proceed under the premise that perhaps we are both of reasonable intelligence?

> *Beat.*

ALICE: Of course.

DAVID: Do we understand each other?

ALICE: Of course.

DAVID: Thank you… Why am I here?

> *Beat.*

ALICE: You have been in an accident…

> DAVID *looks around the room.*

DAVID: An accident… What happened?

ALICE: We're not sure… We need to run a series of tests, David. In order to find out…

DAVID: Tests…

ALICE: Yes.

DAVID: How long will they take?

ALICE: How do you mean?

DAVID: How long will they take...? What time is it?

> ALICE *checks her watch. Beat.*

ALICE: It's 5:00 p.m.

DAVID: Okay. Good... So a series of tests...

> DAVID *stands and looks at his bare feet for a moment.*

ALICE: ... Yes.

> ALICE *makes a note.*

DAVID: Why?

ALICE: Well, as I said—

DAVID: No I understand what you said, Alice, I'm just at a loss to see why I need to / undergo—

ALICE: / Because, David, you have—

DAVID: When I feel perfectly fine why do I need to undergo, be subjected to, be made to / jump through—

ALICE: / David, it's a—

DAVID: This series of 'tests'. And hence my question. Why?

> *Beat.*

ALICE: ... It's a requirement.

> *Pause.*

DAVID: A requirement. A requirement of yours?

ALICE: A requirement.

DAVID: You are just doing your job...

ALICE: Yes.

DAVID: Alright... I understand that. I can understand that.

> *Pause.* DAVID *stares at her.*

ALICE: Fine. So... names... I'm Alice—

DAVID: Will they take long? These tests? Will they take long?

ALICE: Why, David?

DAVID: Because I have somewhere to be.

ALICE: ... It depends.

DAVID: On what?

ALICE: On what the tests reveal.

Pause. DAVID *looks at her.*

DAVID: Fine, so I am David. Yes. Next?

ALICE: Yes. And I am?

Pause.

DAVID: You are Alice, Alice…

ALICE: Yes. So if you were to try and—?

DAVID: Alice in Wonderland. I would associate your name with something else, yes?

ALICE: Yes. Good.

DAVID: Good.

ALICE: You can associate a new memory, the memory of me with an older memory of something familiar. And what if my name was Wendy?

Pause.

DAVID: Is Alice not your name?

ALICE: Alice is my name but for the sake of argument.

DAVID: Wendy…? I don't know… Wendy in Wonderland.

Pause.

ALICE: Let's try a mnemonic device then. Do you know what a /mnemonic is?

DAVID: / Yes.

ALICE: … So?

Pause.

DAVID: So what?

ALICE: For my name.

DAVID: Alice or Wendy?

ALICE: Alice.

DAVID: I know your name, Alice. It's on your name tag. Jesus Christ, I think we've established your name.

ALICE: Let's just try.

Pause.

DAVID: All Ice.

Pause.

ALICE: Good, David, poetics... both aural and visual... but not a mnemonic.

DAVID: Well... At Least I Can Entertain.

ALICE: —

Pause.

DAVID: Do I get a tick for that, do you think, Alice?

Pause. He gets up and looks about the room. Pokes his head into the bathroom.

Apologies, Alice, that was rude of me, it's just I'm a little... a little confused, Alice.

ALICE: Yes?

DAVID: Why am I here...?

Pause.

ALICE: ... There was an incident, David.

DAVID: An incident? What incident?

ALICE: In which you lost time...

Beat.

DAVID: You mean I... I fainted...? Like a dizzy spell?

Beat.

ALICE: We're not sure.

DAVID: But I'm okay? You said I was okay.

ALICE: Yes, David, you're okay.

Beat. DAVID *smiles.*

DAVID: Okay. Alright. I see. I see... So these tests are simply an... an... an insurance for /

ALICE: / They're a—

DAVID: / A protocol, yes? I understand. A procedure, Alice? For the hospital? Because you need to /

ALICE: / They're to assess your—

DAVID: / I see, yes. Of course. With anything like this, no matter how minor, no matter how trivial, you still need to /... to indemnify—

ALICE: / No, David—

DAVID: / To cover your, to uphold, I see, before you can release your charge...

ALICE: Yes…?

DAVID: Before you can inflict me back into the world.

ALICE: No, David.

DAVID: You need to… I see. Can I help you here, Alice…? And then perhaps you could help me? You see my time is very precious… and I need to get back to my work, so if you need my… if you have a form which needs my… I am happy to waive whatever in order to indemnify the hospital because you see, I'm fine, just fine and… I'd like to leave now. [*Beat.*] And I do appreciate your duty of care and presumably what the capable staff here have done for me, you have all been very kind and helpful, however they do seem to have misplaced my clothes and my other belongings. Could you see where they have placed those things, Alice?… Because I'd like to leave…

> *Pause.*

ALICE: Where would you go?

DAVID: I have an engagement. I have to be somewhere…

ALICE: It's not possible I'm afraid, David.

DAVID: No?

ALICE: No. It's not possible.

DAVID: Anything is possible where pressure is applied, Alice. I'd like to speak to your superior…

ALICE: My…?

DAVID: Your senior, the person in charge… You see, I am, right now, right this instant, in the middle of a very pressing circumstance which requires my attention. And I'm not going to forgo that responsibility because you are required to tick boxes. So I'm leaving…

ALICE: That's not possible, David.

DAVID: Not possible…?

ALICE: No.

DAVID: Why…? Because I've had a dizzy spell? Jesus Christ.

> *He jumps up and does star jumps directly in front of her. The following overlaps:*

ALICE: David, look… I'm not capable / of… this is beyond my jurisdiction… this is simply a requirement of—

> ALICE *closes her computer.*

DAVID: / Look… fine… spatial acuity—

ALICE: Sit down, David, please. / David, sit down please. C'mon…

DAVID: / Can touch my toes… walk in a straight line while touching my nose with both left and right arm at full extension, / everything in working order—

ALICE: / No, David, you suffered a—

He stops and recites the following quickly:

DAVID: You are not wrong, who deem
That my days have been a dream,
Yet if hope has flown away
In a night, or in a day,
In a vision, or in none,
Is it therefore the less gone?
All that we see or seem
Is but a dream within a dream.
Now where are my goddamn clothes?

ALICE: Edgar Allan Poe.

DAVID: Very good, we find common ground, you like poetry, good for you.

ALICE: I like Poe.

DAVID taps his head.

DAVID: Learnt that by rote when I was twelve. So let me sign the waiver because I'm leaving… Do you understand? I have to get back to my work…

ALICE: What's the second verse?

DAVID: Oh, come on! Brain fine. Me go. Where are my clothes?

ALICE: You seem agitated David.

DAVID: Yes I am agitated. I would like to leave.

Pause. DAVID *moves towards the door.* ALICE *furtively looks up at the CCTV camera.*

ALICE: Sit down, David… Come on… sit down.

DAVID tries to exit but there's no door handle.

DAVID: Where's the…? Why is this locked? Alice?

ALICE: Why don't you sit down, David?

DAVID: Open the door.

ALICE: I can't do that I'm afraid.

DAVID turns around, looks at the ground and thinks. ALICE watches him.

David?

He looks about the room and then at his pyjamas. Finally he stares at ALICE without moving for fifteen seconds.

DAVID: Who are you?

ALICE finally breathes. She gets up and takes DAVID by the elbow and guides him towards the bed.

ALICE: Why don't you sit on the bed, David, you'll be more comfortable.

She then moves toward the door looking up toward the CCTV camera as she does.

I'm Alice… Do you mind if I sit?

DAVID gestures for her to sit. She does.

Thank you. I'm here to help.

Pause.

DAVID: Where am I?

ALICE: You're in a hospital, David.

DAVID: Hospital?

ALICE: Yes.

DAVID: Where are my clothes?

ALICE: It's all being looked after, David.

DAVID: Have I been in some kind of accident?

Pause. ALICE sits back in her chair and considers.

ALICE: No. You just had a dizzy spell so we're just making sure that everything is in order… You're safe here… How are you feeling?

DAVID: Well… I feel fine… just fine. Just a little…

ALICE: David, I need to ask you some questions. Yes?

DAVID looks around the room, uncertain.

Yes?

DAVID: Okay.

ALICE: What's the last thing you remember?

DAVID: I was in my office… I was working in my office.

ALICE opens her computer and hits a button.

ALICE: One moment… alright. You were in your office, working, doing what?

DAVID: … Finalising a brief. Why?

ALICE: Were you alone in the office?

DAVID: … No, I was with my associate. He was helping me with the brief.

ALICE: And what is his name?

DAVID: Michael Perry.

> DAVID *gets up and looks around the room over the following, taking it in for the first time.*

ALICE: And what else?

DAVID: … I was on the phone.

ALICE: Who to?

DAVID: My wife.

ALICE: You were on the phone to your wife… What were you discussing?

DAVID: Plans for the weekend. It's our wedding anniversary tomorrow. We're going to go away tonight but I was behind on this brief.

ALICE: Where were you going to go?

DAVID: We have a house. Up in the hills, on a lake. … Are you recording this?

ALICE: Yes.

DAVID: Why?

ALICE: It's a protocol, David…

> DAVID *nods.*

You were meant to be going away but you were running late…?

> DAVID *looks up at the high windows.*

DAVID: … So I said for her to go up on her own, I'd put this brief to bed, come up first thing tomorrow morning.

ALICE: And then what happened?

> DAVID *thinks.*

DAVID: I hung up and… and then I must have… What time is it?

ALICE: Just after five.

> *Beat.*

DAVID: Look, you know what… is this… is this going to take long?

ALICE: I'll try to make it as brief as possible for you, David.

Pause. DAVID *sits on the bed.*

How did this happen, do you think?

DAVID: ... I don't know... [*He shrugs.*] ... I have no idea. I was in my office, on the phone to my wife, and now I'm here... I don't know... Ask my associate... Ask my wife...

ALICE *blinks. Pause.*

I assume she's aware that I'm in here, yes...?

Beat.

ALICE: Okay, David, my task here is to—

DAVID: Wait a minute... Ask my wife...

ALICE: It's alright, David. I'm here to help.

DAVID: I want to speak with my wife. Where's the phone? [*He looks about the room.*] Can I use your phone please?

ALICE: No... Look, David, I need you to sit down and—

DAVID: Has she been informed? Does she know I'm here? I would like to speak with my wife. [*Beat.*] If I do not use your phone then I will walk out of here and use the public phone in the corridor. I am asking you politely before I invoke some less friendly, more litigious terminologies. I'm not sure if you are aware but I am a lawyer and right now you are obstructing me and this hospital has neglected to inform next of kin. [*Pause.*] May I use your phone? Alice... Please.

Pause.

ALICE: Of course.

She hands her phone to him. He dials and wanders over to the bed. Voicemail.

DAVID: [*into the phone*] It's me, I'm on someone else's phone so don't call back on it... Look, you might already be driving up to the house but there's been a... I don't quite know what's happened... I'm at a hospital but I'm absolutely fine. I've had some kind of a faint spell at the office and they're giving me the once-over here but I'm going to go there now and finish this brief so that it doesn't eat into the anniversary... I'll call you from there... It's all fine, but if I don't speak to you tonight I'll see you in the morning... [*He hangs up, passes her the phone and sits down.*] So... now if you're done then I think that this, Alice... whatever this procedure of yours is, is over

and I'd like to go back to my room please and I would like my clothes
and my other possessions returned...

ALICE: This is your room, David.

> DAVID *looks about.*

DAVID: Where are my clothes?

ALICE: What do you think is going on, David?

DAVID: —

ALICE: What do you think is going on?

> ALICE *pushes a file across the table toward him.*

DAVID: What's this?

ALICE: A medical report... on you.

> *Beat. He doesn't pick it up.*

DAVID: On me?

ALICE: Yes... What day is it today, David?

> *Beat.*

DAVID: Friday the fifteenth...

ALICE: The day before your anniversary?

DAVID: ... Yes.

ALICE: Today is Saturday the twenty-third... You have been with us now
for seven days, David... Do you understand...?

> DAVID *slowly opens the medical report. He begins to read it.*

You've been involved in a serious accident, David, in which you have
lost time... David...?

> DAVID *flips a page. Then stares, frozen, at* ALICE. *Pause.*

DAVID: Where am I?

> *Beat.*

ALICE: [*to herself*] Shit... [*Then:*] I'm Alice... I'm here to help... you're
safe here... safe...

SCENE TWO

*We hear the P.A. distantly. It's now the following day, October twenty-
fourth at 4:00 p.m. It's raining gently outside.* ALICE *stands by the table
watching* DAVID *for a moment.*

ALICE: How are you feeling today?

DAVID: Fine… Will these tests take long?

ALICE: No they won't take long, Mr Rail. We're just waiting on a few results. They shouldn't be long. We'll have you home in good time.

Beat. DAVID *looks up at the high windows.*

DAVID: What time is it?

ALICE: Are you concerned about your brief?

DAVID: … Yes…

ALICE: Mr Perry called about this and he wanted to assure you that it was under control…

Pause.

DAVID: Did he…? Have we met before? [*Pause.*] Because you seem familiar.

ALICE: Do you feel as if we have met before?

DAVID: —

ALICE: … Perhaps I have one of those faces…

Pause.

DAVID: And my wife… is she…?

ALICE: She's on her way here now. To pick you up…

Beat.

DAVID: Good…

Beat.

ALICE: I understand that you're a lawyer, Mr Rail… It's on your admission form.

Beat.

DAVID: I knew an Alice once.

ALICE: Yes?

DAVID: … Not the golden locks and blue skirt you'd expect. A single mother of five who had killed her last three… Hands like talons… Eyes like chainsaws.

ALICE: I remember this. She drowned them in a lake…

DAVID: The pinnacle of survivalism. Alice Bilkington…

ALICE: What made her do it, do you think?

DAVID: I don't know… Time multiplied by life…

Beat.

ALICE: You prosecuted her?

DAVID *nods.*

And you're not sure why she did it?

DAVID: That wasn't within my purview. I just had to prove that she did it.

ALICE: And did she?

DAVID: She never denied it. Defence, however, argued automatism. That it was all a compulsion without intent.

ALICE: And you won that case?

DAVID: Yes.

Pause.

ALICE: As a lawyer… I hope you don't mind me asking… But what does it take to be successful, do you think, Mr Rail? Do you have to think like a criminal? Is that it?

DAVID: No.

ALICE: What do you have to do to win then?

Beat.

DAVID: Make sure you have the dominant narrative.

ALICE: The dominant…?

DAVID: It's about always owning the dominant narrative… and leading the jury to the most logical conclusion.

Beat. ALICE *smiles.*

ALICE: Like a writer… You must enjoy your work, Mr Rail.

DAVID: … Yes.

ALICE: What is it you like about it most?

DAVID: The salary.

ALICE: Surely that's not why…

DAVID: A court of law is just a machine that makes logic… where evidence is contested according to logic. And logic is… sometimes beautiful.

ALICE: Is it not about truth? Contesting truth?

DAVID: Truth is about plausibility but logic is undeniable. Crime operates on logic. Action and causality… Means, motive and opportunity. Truth on the other hand operates on the less empirical planes of belief and language. Truth… language… can be paradoxical… a matrix of untested assumptions. Logic on the other hand is like a knife.

ALICE: Like the 'Liar's Paradox'.

DAVID: —

ALICE: There are variations on it, but it's this: I say, 'I always lie'. If this is true then this statement is false because I have just stated a truth. If this statement is false, i.e. I *am* lying, then it paradoxically proves it's true and so on and so on. A never-ending paradox... unsolvable... But if you have to *own* the narrative then you would have to deploy language, yes?

DAVID: It's all we have. But you do it with logic and deductive reasoning. You live life with language, but go to court with logic.

> *Pause.*

ALICE: Do you attract enemies doing what you do?

DAVID: ... I'm not alone in that.

ALICE: And what of the legal fraternity itself?

> DAVID *smiles.*

DAVID: I don't know who it is you've been talking with, but it's within that exact fraternity in which a lawyer makes his greatest enemies.

ALICE: And what do you have to do about these enemies?

> *Beat.*

DAVID: How are those tests results getting along?

> *Beat.*

ALICE: Not long now...

DAVID: So I take it you're a novice when it comes to the inner workings of our gallant legal system?

ALICE: Yes.

DAVID: So what do I do about enemies?

ALICE: Yes.

DAVID: It's an adversarial system. It's about survival. To the top end of town you wear the mask of civility and with members of the criminal class it's no different. Logical members of a logical society sharing their own set of logical rules, the pre-eminent one being golden. Some people choose to put their trust in the leveraged threat of revenge, but again it's all predicated on the logic of survival.

ALICE: ... Why would they *want* revenge, do you think?

DAVID: Revenge? Why does anyone? We're a social species where everything is weighed upon the basis of trust. And when that trust is

betrayed, well… it's the three steps… Trust, Betrayal, Revenge…
but it always begins with trust.

Beat.

ALICE: Who is Reynolds?

Pause.

DAVID: Reynolds?
ALICE: Do you know anyone by that name?
DAVID: No… I don't think so. Why?
ALICE: When you were brought in you repeatedly called out that name…
Reynolds…? Mr Rail…? You were calling out Reynolds…

DAVID *looks about the room. Then to* ALICE*:*

DAVID: Who are you?
ALICE: I'm Alice…

SCENE THREE

*The P.A. can be heard faintly in the corridor. Time has shifted. It's now
two days later, 11:00 a.m., October twenty-sixth. Sun streams in through
the windows.* DAVID *is now seated at the table.* ALICE *stands near the
door.*

ALICE: You're safe here.
DAVID: —
ALICE: Do you mind if I sit?

DAVID *gestures for her to take a seat.*

I'm here to help.
DAVID: … I've been in an accident of some kind?
ALICE: Yes.
DAVID: What happened?
ALICE: We're hoping you can help us find out. [*Pause. She opens her
computer and presses a button.*] You understand that this is being
recorded?
DAVID: Recorded?
ALICE: Would you like to see the waiver you signed?
DAVID: … No.

Beat. He looks around the room and up at the windows.

ALICE: Tell me, David, what's the last thing you remember?

DAVID: I woke up.

ALICE: And?

DAVID: Here I am.

ALICE: Then before that?

DAVID: Nothing. A dream…

ALICE: What was the dream about?

> DAVID *shakes his head.*

DAVID: … Can't remember…

ALICE: Try…

DAVID: Don't know… a room, a doorway… there was a man… I don't know… [*Pause.*] Have I met you before? [*Pause.*] Because you seem familiar.

ALICE: — [*Pause.*] There was an event, David… an event… in which you suffered a brain injury. [*Beat.*] We think you have some damage to the hippocampus… there's two of them, left and right. They're like an exchange box that directs short- and long-term memory. As far as we can tell yours has taken something of an insult.

DAVID: An insult…

> *Beat.*

ALICE: Your long-term memory appears perfectly functional, your sense of identity, your comprehension etcetera, however you seem unable to retain new memories, David. You have what is called anterograde amnesia…

> *Pause.*

DAVID: I see… As a result of this… injury?

ALICE: Yes.

> *Pause.* DAVID *gets up and looks about the room.*

DAVID: How long have I been here?

ALICE: Ten days.

> *Beat.*

DAVID: My wife… I'd like to speak to my wife.

ALICE: I'll see what I can do…

> *Beat.*

DAVID: … What's the prognosis?

ALICE: There are some signs of improvement. You're finding new pathways. Neurons that weren't talking to each other are now beginning to talk. In cases such as this there's a reasonable chance of recovery. The duration and lucidity of your short-term memory is getting longer and more consistent.

DAVID: But I can't retain these new memories?

ALICE: Not yet. No.

DAVID: So what you're saying is that… in a few minutes I'll 'wake up' with no memory of this…?

ALICE: Given time, the brain can re-map itself. You are developing what is called 'island memories'. Patients with your condition can begin to recall episodic memories… post trauma…

> *She goes to her computer and presses a number of keys. Her computer starts playing a recording from a previous session.*

ALICE: *'Is there anything that is upsetting you here, David? Here in the hospital.'*

> *Pause.*

DAVID: *'The night nurse… when you ring the buzzer…'*

ALICE: *'When you ring the buzzer…?'*

DAVID: *'She's brusque… turns the lights on… says things.'*

ALICE: *'Like what? What does she say to you?'*

> *Beat.*

DAVID: *'… She calls me a liar… she says I'm her favourite liar…'*

ALICE: *'What does she look like, David?'*

> ALICE *presses a key on the computer. The recording stops.*

ALICE: Two days ago you described one of the night nurses here, Eleanor. This is an 'island memory'… post trauma. You are using the unaffected parts of your brain to hold a narrative of Eleanor.

DAVID: But I don't remember it now…

ALICE: It's in there somewhere… in the labyrinth.

DAVID: I don't understand… How did this happen to me?

> *Pause.*

ALICE: Do you trust me, David? [*Pause.*] David… on the *sixteenth* of October you were found, bleeding from a laceration to the head by a roadside… disorientated… [*Pause.*] Do you believe what I've just told you, David…? Do you understand?

DAVID: I understand… I understand what you are telling me but I…

ALICE: But what, David?

DAVID: … I don't feel… it feels like… like you're lying to me.

ALICE: I'm here to help you, David. You need to trust me.

> DAVID *shrugs and looks about, lost.*

I understand that it must be very difficult for you.

> *Pause.*

DAVID: … I was working in my office…

ALICE: Yes, David.

DAVID: … And then I wake up here… with this… condition… like a… a… a perpetual hypothesis… Have you told me this before?

ALICE: About your condition…? Yes.

> *Pause.*

DAVID: And what was my reaction?

ALICE: You said that you felt as if I was lying to you.

> *Pause.* DAVID *goes to the door. There's no door handle. It's locked.*

DAVID: Why is this locked?

ALICE: For your safety, David… There is a buzzer by the bed if you need anything.

> DAVID *slowly crosses to the bed and sits, lost in thought.*

… I have something for you, David.

> *She takes out a journal with a pen tethered to it and slides it across the table to him.*

DAVID: What's this?

ALICE: To help you… to help you keep track of your thoughts. I want you to know that you can trust me, David, and that I'm here to do whatever I can to help you.

> ALICE *takes out* DAVID*'s reading glasses and places them on top of the journal.* ALICE *closes her computer and gets up to leave. They share a silent look for a moment. She looks up at the CCTV camera and presses a buzzer by the door.*

DAVID: Why is she calling me a liar?

ALICE: Eleanor?

DAVID: Why is she calling me a liar?

ALICE: I suspect she's being playful with you. Your name is posted on the outside of your door. It's reflected in the corridor window opposite at night when Eleanor is on shift... Liar is a palindrome... of your name...

> *There is the sound of the door being unlocked.* ALICE *exits.* DAVID *slowly puts on his glasses, opens the journal, thinks, and begins to write in it very carefully. After a moment he looks over to the bed then turns his gaze to the CCTV camera. He closes the journal, gets up and goes into the bathroom. There is the sound of a tap running. The light in the high windows outside fades to night.*

SCENE FOUR

DAVID *enters from the bathroom, drying his face on a towel. He looks about the dim room. He puts the towel in the bathroom.*

DAVID: Hello...? Hello? [*He moves to the bed.*] Hello?

> *He sits on the bed. He looks up into the corner of the room and sees the CCTV camera. He gets up and vaguely waves into it. He sees the door and examines it. It's locked. He tries to force it with his shoulder, then again with more force until he notices the intercom next to it. He presses it.*

Hello... hello...

> *Nothing. He tries the door again even harder. He bangs loudly on the door.*

Hey...! Hey...! Hello!

> *He presses his ear to the upstage wall and listens. He taps on the wall three times and waits for a response. Nothing. He sees the buzzer next to the bed. He presses it several times. He goes to the door and bangs on it.*

Hello...? Hello...? What is going on? I'm in here! Hey! I'm in here!

> *Then he notices the journal sitting on the table. He picks it up, recognises his glasses and reads. There's a knock on the door. He freezes. From outside we hear muffled voices. The door is unlocked and opens.* ALICE *steps in.*

ALICE: Hello, David.

> *Pause.*

DAVID: Who are you?

ALICE: You're safe here, David… I'm Alice… I'm here to help.

> *Lights fade to black.*

SCENE FIVE

The light in the windows blinks to early morning daylight. October twenty-seventh. ALICE *is unpacking her computer and laying out some images on the table.* DAVID *is sitting on the bed flicking through several pages of the journal.* ALICE *sits as* DAVID *puts down the journal, moves to the table and begins looking at the images. He picks up a photograph. He looks at it.*

ALICE: David…? Describe what you see.

DAVID: … A boy, sitting in the doorway of an old cabin. There are no windows on the cabin… Daytime, but dark inside… dark inside the doorway.

ALICE: What's the narrative…? Tell me a story of it.

DAVID: … He's poor… from a poor family… no shoes on… He's waiting.

ALICE: For what?

DAVID: It's daytime. Sunny outside. He should be outside. But he's not allowed. Like he's been told he can't go outside so he's sitting on the threshold. Looking at what he's missing out on.

ALICE: Who said he's not to go outside?

DAVID: … The person who's taking the photograph.

ALICE: The person taking the photograph? Why has he been told he can't go outside?

DAVID: He's done something wrong, I suppose.

ALICE: … Does he understand that?

DAVID: No. He just wants to be outside. In the light…

> DAVID *hands it back.* ALICE *hands him an illustration.*

ALICE: Now this one.

> DAVID *looks at it.*

DAVID: It's an illustration, Victorian era… A woman covering her face with one hand in the foreground, behind her a doorway to a small room... A man lying fully clothed on the bed in the background, unconscious or asleep... An empty bottle next to the bed...

ALICE: So what do you think is happening?

Beat.

DAVID: Well, she's looking down... covering herself in shame. She's stepped out of the room to do this. Either she doesn't want him to see this guilt or...

ALICE: Or what?

DAVID: Why is he fully dressed...? The room is small, like a cabin on a ship... But there's daylight coming through the portal... What has she done?

ALICE: What do you think?

DAVID: They're on a ship... a journey... A honeymoon. He's asleep... unaware. The bottle...

ALICE: Yes?

DAVID: An empty bottle. It's sitting in a basin... It's not what it contained but more what it doesn't contain now... now it's empty.

Pause.

ALICE: What do you think is going on?

DAVID: She has... she realises that she no longer loves this man. She is trying to work out what to do next.

ALICE: What do you think she will do next?

DAVID: ... She'll plan her escape...

He hands the picture back. She passes another. He looks at it.

It's a house. Out in the country... A painting of a house in a snowstorm. It has a face. The house has a face.

ALICE: Describe the face. What kind of face is it?

DAVID: ... Imbecilic... mad... The windows are empty-eyed.

He places the picture back on the table.

ALICE: Does anyone live there?

DAVID: No. No-one lives there. It's empty. The house is just a thing in itself.

DAVID *goes to the bed and makes a note in his journal.*

ALICE: Tell me about your house... on the lake.

Pause. DAVID *continues to write through the following:*

DAVID: It's isolated… There's a long dirt driveway off the main road. All deserted… we're on the eastern side of the lake… It's deep, never been plumbed… Formed from a collapsed caldera 250 million years ago… No-one around for miles… you get the occasional hunter… It's high country… Gothic Revival… built in the twenties by a pig farmer… The remnants of an orchard, various crumbling outhouses… an overgrown maze. Nothing around for miles. We were planning to go up there for our anniversary…

ALICE: Oh… you and your wife?

DAVID: Yes.

ALICE: You'd hear a car approaching? It's that quiet…?

Pause. DAVID *looks up.*

DAVID: Yes.

DAVID *makes further notes.* ALICE *looks at his medical report.*

ALICE: You don't have any children.

DAVID: No.

ALICE: Was that a choice you made…? You and your wife?

DAVID: Sarah…? We considered it for some time… she's some years younger than me… but never found a reason.

ALICE: … Are they not a continuance… another chapter in the narrative… an extension of oneself?

DAVID: You mean genetic continuance…? With the world's population ballooning into chaos the last thing we need is to propagate yet another soul, not the least one with the genetic predisposition of a lawyer.

ALICE *smiles.*

Or perhaps we do…

ALICE: Was it because of the field you work in…? Having to confront what you do… is that why you didn't have children, do you think?

DAVID: No.

ALICE: Why then?

DAVID: … Perhaps it's not always a choice, Alice…

Pause.

ALICE: Jung proposed another kind of continuance… a kind of genetic memory, the collective unconscious… Inherited psychic data linking us to each other and to our past...? Based upon the archetypes. The Animus, the Anima... the Shadow.

DAVID: The Shadow?

ALICE: He thought that the Shadow was the psychic remnants of the saurian tail that we discarded when we climbed out of the trees... the reservoir of human darkness. The Shadow presents itself in dreams as a projection... a projection of the dreamer... in an opening of some kind... a dark figure in a doorway... [*Pause.*] Did you have a difficult childhood?

DAVID: I thought this was to assess my condition, Alice? Why do I feel like it's now taken a sinister turn and become a psychological assessment?

ALICE: Apologies, David. I'll explain. This is just a standard procedure. I'm establishing a baseline.

DAVID: Of what?

ALICE: Of your episodic memory, to see how well you can recall past events... especially those linked to strong emotion. Depression in early childhood can be a precursor to a range of conditions relating to memory. I'm trying to see if there are any pre-conditions that I need to take into account. Did you ever, do you think, suffer depression as a child, David?

> *Beat.*

DAVID: No.

ALICE: Tell me something from your childhood. An event...

DAVID: Like what?

ALICE: What was your proudest moment, David?

> DAVID *closes the journal.*

DAVID: Proudest moment?

ALICE: Something that you felt was an achievement... Whatever springs...

> *Pause.*

DAVID: At school... I was, twelve... thirteen, and... I had a nemesis... the type who hits puberty young. It's lunchtime... we're loitering outside. He's been at me for weeks. Hazing me in the grand tradition... Right toward the end of lunch he starts in again. Calling me names.

ALICE: Like what?

DAVID: … I don't remember

ALICE: Why was he calling you names?

DAVID: Alice… please… does everything have to have a causality…? Alright… He was bored and frustrated and diverting himself by establishing a pecking order thus engendering himself with a sense of worth that had not been provided to him by either the school, his parents or his own chaotic mind. Now would you like me to proceed with the anecdote?

She smiles.

ALICE: Of course…

DAVID: So… without thinking… I turn, grab him by the shirt and I knee him, hard as I can in his pubescent testicles and he goes down like the proverbial. The lunch bell rings, like at the end of a fight, and I walk back to class, sit in my seat and look out the window to where, there he is, still curled in a ball, all foetal, like the oversized baby he was. Never bothered me again… nor anyone else.

ALICE: And that made you proud?

DAVID: —

Pause.

ALICE: Was it impulsive, do you think? Hurting him like that?

DAVID: Hurting him…? I was asserting myself, Alice. Call it an act of self-preservation.

ALICE: Survival?

DAVID: Yes.

ALICE: Your first experience of doling out justice, David?

DAVID *looks at the journal.*

DAVID: Perhaps… I take it you've never reacted impulsively…?

ALICE: When I was twelve I broke a girl's jaw…

Beat.

DAVID: Why?

ALICE: She'd lied to me…

DAVID: About a boy?

ALICE: I'll let you fill in the blanks…

Pause.

DAVID: … Can I ask you a question?

ALICE: Yes, David.

DAVID: Are you a doctor?

Beat.

ALICE: … Yes.

DAVID: Of what?

Pause.

ALICE: Psychology…

DAVID: You're a psychologist. [*He makes a note.*] I see… and you're recording these sessions?

ALICE: Yes… It's a legal requirement… because of this condition…

Pause.

DAVID: I was found… on the sixteenth… *non compos mentis*… wandering around…

ALICE: Yes.

DAVID *writes this down.*

DAVID: How long had I been missing?

ALICE: About fourteen hours.

DAVID: I had been reported missing?

ALICE: … Yes.

DAVID: … By my wife… Sarah?

Beat.

ALICE: No.

DAVID: No…? By whom then…?

ALICE: —

DAVID: Why didn't my wife report it?

Pause.

ALICE: … David… we don't feel that you're ready…

Beat.

DAVID: Alice? Why didn't my wife—?

He moves across the room and closes her computer.

Why?

ALICE: Sit down, David.

DAVID: Why?

ALICE: You need to sit down… Sit down, David.

> DAVID *sits back on the bed. Beat.*

Your wife is dead. [*Pause.*] She was found in the house… your house… by the lake… [*Pause.*] I'm very sorry, David… I felt that it was best to not inform you of this until… we had hoped that your condition would improve… I'm so sorry…

DAVID: … I don't…? She's dead? My wife is dead? Sarah is dead?

ALICE: Yes, David…

DAVID: What do you mean she was found? Did I find her?

> *Pause.*

ALICE: The police…

> *Pause.*

DAVID: No.

ALICE: David—

DAVID: I don't believe… I want to go there… to the house… I want to see the house.

ALICE: I'm sorry, David, but that's not possible.

DAVID: I want to see for myself.

> *Pause.*

ALICE: Your house was destroyed by fire. Your wife was in it… An autopsy revealed she'd been stabbed seventeen times… I'm very sorry for your loss, David… I'm very sorry…

> DAVID *picks up the journal and moves to the table, pushing the pictures to one side. He begins to write and then, without looking up, says:*

DAVID: Get out.

> *He continues making hurried notes.* ALICE *watches him as she packs up her things. She moves to the door and presses the intercom. She turns to look at him. He's stopped writing but is reading instead.*

ALICE: David…? Are you alright…?

> *He looks up. He looks around the room.*

DAVID: What's… what's going on? [*He looks back at the journal.*] What's this… what does this mean?

ALICE: David?

DAVID: I don't understand… What is…? Who are you?

ALICE: I'm Alice… Alice… I'm here to help you.

DAVID: What's going on? What is going on?

ALICE: It's okay… You're okay, David… you're okay…

    Lights crossfade to night-time.

SCENE SIX

DAVID *sits on the bed with his legs dangling limply.* ALICE *watches him from near the door.* DAVID *slowly reads from the journal.*

DAVID: 'I'm sitting at the table. There's a man on the bed. I call out to him but he doesn't move. I keep calling but he keeps on sleeping. I go over and prod him on the shoulder and he moans… and I suddenly realise… and I suddenly understand that I am in his dream… And I'm only here as long as he continues to sleep and that if he wakes up, I'll disappear… And just then there's a knocking at the door. And it gets louder and louder and I'm trying to tell whoever it is to shut up and go away because this man will wake up and I'll disappear but they keep pounding at the door. And then I look back at the bed and he's gone… the knocking stops… I hear the tap go on in the bathroom. I move towards the bathroom and look around the door and… he's washing his face in the sink, very slowly… and then when he stands up he just disappears… and then there's just me… me and the mirror. I stand there for a long time… the tap still running. I wash my face, I turn the tap off and go back into the room there he is… sitting down at the table… writing… He gets up and moves to the bed and gets in… All curled up. Facing the wall. Asleep. And it starts all over again.' [*He flicks through the journal then drops it onto the floor.*] This is real, isn't it…? I mean all of this… this is real… isn't it…?

ALICE: David…

    DAVID *curls into a ball on the bed facing the wall.*

DAVID: I want to be alone.

ALICE: Of course.

> *She grabs her things and knocks on the door. It's opened and she exits, the door closing behind her. After a moment* DAVID *gets up, picks up the journal and reads. He looks up at the CCTV camera. He puts the journal back on the table and goes into the bathroom. We hear the sound of the tap running.*

SCENE SEVEN

Daylight spills through the high windows. It's the afternoon of the next day, October twenty-eighth. DAVID *is pacing alone. After a moment he goes to the journal and makes a note. There is a knock on the door. He closes the journal and hides it under his pillow and sits on the bed. There is the sound of the door being unlocked.* ALICE *enters and closes the door.*

ALICE: Hello, David. How are you feeling today?

> DAVID *doesn't respond.* ALICE *moves to the table and takes out her computer. He barely looks at her.*

DAVID: You Alice?

ALICE: Yes.

DAVID: You are my doctor?

ALICE: Yes.

DAVID: How long have I been here?

ALICE: You've been with us for a little while now.

DAVID: … The date?

ALICE: The twenty-eighth.

DAVID: Of…?

ALICE: October.

DAVID: And I was admitted on the sixteenth? Saturday the sixteenth?

ALICE: On the sixteenth… yes.

DAVID: Did you give me something?

ALICE: Did I…? Yes, I did.

DAVID: What… what was it?

> *Pause.*

ALICE: I gave you a journal… a writing journal.

> DAVID *pulls the journal out.*

DAVID: You gave me this?

ALICE: Yes, David.

DAVID: So I can write down my...

ALICE: ... Yes.

DAVID: My thoughts...? Because I have a type of amnesia... Yes?

Beat.

ALICE: Yes.

DAVID *writes in his journal.*

DAVID: How did I get this...?

ALICE: ... We're not certain... Amnesia has divergent aetiologies and forms. It can be organic, meaning physical, with causes ranging from an epileptic event, blood circulation... toxification of the brain. It can also, in some cases, be caused by a precipitating event such as emotional trauma... a psychic shock...

Beat.

DAVID: ... And there is a police investigation?

ALICE: ... Yes.

Pause.

DAVID: Into the murder of my wife Sarah?

ALICE: Yes.

Beat.

DAVID: ... And she was... she was murdered... in our holiday house on the fifteenth?

Beat.

ALICE: Yes.

DAVID: And have I been interviewed... have I been interviewed by the police?

ALICE: ... Yes. Several times...

DAVID: Were you present at these interviews?

ALICE: ... Because of your condition I was asked to be present, yes.

DAVID: And what did I... what information did I give?

ALICE: You told them that you had arranged to go to the house that evening with your wife but that as you had to work late you had decided that you would meet her up there in the morning instead.

DAVID *writes...*

DAVID: And where was I found on the sixteenth?

ALICE: By a roadside… on the western edge of the lake…

Pause.

DAVID: … I was in my office…

ALICE: That's just the last thing you can recall… the trauma occurred after that…

Pause.

DAVID: And so… and so… when I arrived in the morning I found her…?

ALICE: —

DAVID: And that this is what caused this condition I have… the psychic shock of finding my wife?

ALICE: No… David… This is very difficult… [*Beat.*] At 8:00 p.m. on Friday the fifteenth, CCTV has you driving out of your office building. You purchased a bottle of champagne and flowers from a local store… You were picked up by tollway cameras driving in the direction of the house. You would have arrived at around 10:00 p.m. You texted your wife at approximately 9:30 to tell her you were coming… to not be alarmed if she heard a car approaching… You went to the house, David…

Pause.

DAVID: In what, capacity, was I interviewed by the police?

ALICE: As a suspect… [*Pause.*] Your car was found at the house… parked in the driveway with its lights on and the engine running… it had a hose attached to the exhaust… We think that carbon monoxide poisoning is the contributing factor to your condition… There were gym clothes on the front passenger seat… covered in blood…

Pause. DAVID *writes a detailed note.*

DAVID: Where am I?

ALICE: You are in a secure psychiatric unit.

DAVID: … In a correctional facility?

ALICE: Yes, David.

DAVID *makes another note.*

Do you understand? You have been charged with the murder of your wife.

DAVID *nods. He continues to write.* ALICE *watches him.* DAVID *stops and looks at her. She closes her computer.*

SCENE EIGHT

The light in the windows fades to dusk. It's early evening of October twenty-ninth. The hospital P.A. can be dimly heard along with the light sound of rain. DAVID *sits at the table.* ALICE *stands by the bed.*

ALICE: We can stop if you like...

> DAVID *doesn't move.*

Had there been anything unusual occur recently?

DAVID: No... I mean... there are always the usual stresses. She's a lawyer like...

> *Pause.*

ALICE: We can stop if you like, David...

> DAVID *shakes his head.*

Is that how you met?

DAVID: ... In court... the case was...

> *Beat.*

ALICE: The case was?

DAVID: ... It was a murder... husband kills wife, dresses it up to look like a break-in... the whole thing a scam. There'd been a long history of abuse. Easy. I could have phoned it in... So... There she is. I'd never seen her before... Defence. Day one. She presents, and I... Listen. I don't know why but I'm distracted. Now prosecution... I get up. I mumble something unconvincing in reply. The judge tells me to sit. I sit... and on it goes... When she speaks I'm not making notes. I'm not thinking counterattack. I'm thinking about the timbre of her voice and about the elegance of her argument... her choice of sentence, her vocab, and the air she leaves between thoughts... And her eyes... Which when they do choose to fall upon mine are redolent with logic, inevitability and compassion. The case runs its course. She, against all odds... wins... I offer dinner and she accepts. We sit in this restaurant...

ALICE: What do you talk about?

DAVID: ... Everything... I remember the moment... the moment when I realised that I had fallen in love because... because she said... she said... because I'd asked her, 'What were you like as a young girl?', and she said the strangest, most elliptical thing, she said... 'I can't go back to yesterday because I was a different person then'... We married two months later. We've been married for five years. [*Pause. He seems genuinely upset.*] Why have I done this...? Why I have done this...?

> *Pause.* DAVID *writes in his journal.*

ALICE: It's a quote...

DAVID: What...? What's a quote?

ALICE: 'I can't go back to yesterday because I was a different person then.' I know that simply because of my name.

DAVID: What do you mean?

ALICE: It's from Alice. *Alice in Wonderland.*

SCENE NINE

DAVID *is pacing downstage. Daylight bleeds through the windows. October thirtieth. Afternoon.* ALICE *moves to her laptop and taps the computer—a female voice plays these words:*

AUDIO: ... *bed, rest, awake, tired, dream, wake, snooze, blanket, doze, slumber, snore, nap, peace, yawn, drowsy...*

> ALICE *taps the computer again.*

ALICE: Okay, David...

> DAVID *thinks.* ALICE *writes the responses down on a pad.*

DAVID: Blanket, bed, tired, bed, rest, sleep, snooze, slumber, snore, peace... drowsy... did I say drowsy?

ALICE: No. Any more?

DAVID: Dream... wake... wake... No, that's it. I've missed a few.

ALICE: No, you did very well.

ALICE: We'll try another.

> *She taps the keyboard again.*

AUDIO: ... *thread, pin, eye, sewing, sharp, point, pricked, thimble, haystack, pain, hurt, injection...*

DAVID: Injection. Haystack. Pain, hurt... Thread, stab, eye, point, thimble, needle, pricked, pin. Sewing... wait... Needle...?

ALICE: Yes?

DAVID: Needle... Needle wasn't there, was it?

ALICE: —

DAVID: I know this... this is a test of false... of false memory... of confabulation yes? Needle wasn't there. It's a lure word.

Beat.

ALICE: You're familiar with this test then?

DAVID: This is to assess a propensity for confabulation. For lying...

ALICE: Yes.

DAVID *looks in his journal.*

DAVID: Why?

ALICE: To test the veracity of your condition.

DAVID: To see if I'm malingering...?

ALICE: Yes. I take it you're familiar with this test because you're a lawyer, David?

DAVID: Something like that. But why would you—?

ALICE: You see, David... one of the aspects of my work as a forensic psychologist... my assessment in circumstances such as this, is to conduct field enquiries. You understand?

DAVID: A forensic psychologist?

ALICE: Yes... As a lawyer you represented a client once. Many years ago... There had been a robbery and in the course of your client's escape, he'd been involved in a motorbike accident.

DAVID: ... Yes...

ALICE: And three weeks later when he awoke out of a coma, he claimed he had no memory of the incident.

DAVID: ... Yes.

ALICE: And was acquitted.

DAVID: ... They couldn't establish *mens rea*... and so he was acquitted, yes and... in this instance, he could not remember any of the events around the crime and, as such, prosecution could not establish intent.

ALICE: The point being, David, is that you are familiar with nearly all of the tests I've conducted...? [*Pause.*] Because you would have had to have been to conduct this case. Yes?

DAVID: I suppose.

ALICE: You would need a comprehensive knowledge of malingered memory impairment... to prove that your client was genuine in his claim.

Pause. DAVID *stares at her.*

DAVID: A forensic psychologist...?

ALICE: Did you coach him, David? You understand what I mean by coached? These tests benchmark against the average in order to record the under- or over-exaggeration of claims. We detect 'faking' because they exaggerate their condition. Yes?

DAVID *makes a note in the journal.*

DAVID: As his lawyer I was obliged to give my client every possible advantage but not to the extent that it is in breach of ethical practice.

ALICE: And so...? You didn't coach your client?

DAVID: I instructed him to tell the truth to the best of his ability.

ALICE: Truth. I see. I'm just curious as to why you have not until now recognised these tests that I have been conducting...

Pause.

DAVID: No... what you're wondering is, does my knowledge of these tests give me an unfair advantage in undertaking them to produce a certain result?

ALICE: That depends on whether you're being unfair or not.

Beat.

DAVID: Can I ask you something, Alice? Does your knowledge, as a forensic psychologist, provide you with the same unfair advantage...? Now that you are working for the court?

Pause.

ALICE: I am just trying to provide an outside profile of you prior to the incident.

DAVID: ... And what advantage would it serve for me to 'fake' this condition?

ALICE: Well, you should know this, David... It's called secondary gain. You evade scrutiny... If I determine that you have anterograde amnesia, hence are unfit to stand trial, the charges will be most likely dropped... You escape prosecution.

Pause.

DAVID: … So I go up to the house and for no apparent reason murder my wife. Burn the house down in order to, one would have to assume, destroy the evidence of the crime. Having successfully done this I then decide I will commit suicide instead. I attempt this and then… after a while… wander off into the wilderness. I then *invent* that I can't remember anything, despite the overwhelming evidence, in the hope that I'll avoid prosecution.

ALICE: —

DAVID: Do you see the kink in the logic, Alice?

ALICE: I am not here to ascertain guilt or otherwise, David… I'm simply here at the behest of the court to assess your fitness to stand trial.

DAVID: … What do you think, Alice? Am I malingering?

Pause.

ALICE: Ultimately in regards to guilt or otherwise, the question is irrelevant… because the two options are not mutually exclusive. The fact of amnesia, the fact that you can't recall what happened that night does not logically preclude the possibility of guilt.

DAVID: And if I'm lying, Alice… what am I lying about?

ALICE: I don't know, David… you'd have to tell me.

DAVID: Am I lying about why I did it…? Because I have no fucking idea why I would do this… [*Pause.*] Means, motive, opportunity. There's no motive… [*Pause.*] … Alice…?

ALICE: … The police… the police suspect that she may have been having an affair.

Pause.

DAVID: No… No, I would know… I would know about a thing like that…

ALICE: There were a series of text messages on her phone…

DAVID *slowly makes a note in the journal.*

DAVID: … To whom?

ALICE: They don't know… it was an unlisted number…

Clearly shaken, DAVID *slowly gets up. He looks up to the high windows. After a moment…*

DAVID: Did the police call this number?

ALICE: Yes... it had been deactivated... This must be difficult for you, David... Did you ever suspect...?

DAVID *shakes his head.*

DAVID: So I drove up there... and then... she told me of the affair...
ALICE: —
DAVID: And then I killed her, set fire to the house and then tried to kill myself...
ALICE: Is that what happened, David?

DAVID *sits on the bed and makes a note in the journal.*

DAVID: I would like to speak to a lawyer...
ALICE: Certainly, David, who?
DAVID: Michael Perry.
ALICE: He's unavailable I'm afraid.
DAVID: What do you mean unavailable?
ALICE: You have requested that he represent you a number of times... He has declined...

Pause.

DAVID: ... He thinks I did this...
ALICE: I don't know his reasons...

Pause.

DAVID: Then I'll represent myself... I have nothing more to say...

DAVID *makes a note in the book.* ALICE *packs up and leaves. When she is gone* DAVID *closes the journal. He goes and sits back on the bed. He puts the journal under the pillow then turns around facing the wall and curls up on the bed and quietly sobs. The light through the windows fades to darkness, then the lights snap off in the room. The red light on the CCTV camera blinks away.*

SCENE TEN

ALICE *is standing by the door and* DAVID *is sitting on the bed. Morning. October thirty-first.*

DAVID: Are you Alice?
ALICE: Yes, David. How are you feeling today?

DAVID: What's the date?

ALICE: It's the thirty-first.

DAVID takes out the book and makes a note. He then turns back a page and reads.

DAVID: Last time we met was yesterday?

ALICE: Yes.

DAVID: [*reading*] 'What was the last text that my wife sent to the unlisted number?'

ALICE: What are you doing, David?

DAVID flicks back through the journal and reads.

DAVID: [*reading*] 'I am acting as my own counsel as I have been charged with the murder of Sarah Rail.' My wife. [*Reading on*] 'And as such I have a legal right to access information relating to the case against me.'

Pause.

ALICE: This is insane.

DAVID: [*reading*] 'What was the last text that my wife sent to the unlisted number?' [*Pause.*] What was the last text that my wife sent to the unlisted number?

ALICE puts her bag down.

ALICE: I don't have access to that information, David.

DAVID flicks back through the journal. Then looks up at her.

DAVID: If you are testing the veracity of my condition then all pertinent facts would have been made available to you by the police in order to conduct your assessment. What was the last text that my wife sent to the unlisted number?

Beat.

ALICE: 'Need to see you. Something has happened. Meet me at the house on the lake. Text yes or no.'

DAVID: And the response?

ALICE: 'Yes.'

DAVID makes a note.

DAVID: And that was it? No further texts?

ALICE: Only yours…

> DAVID *gets up and paces.* ALICE *watches him.*

David, I'm sorry but… I've come to say goodbye… I've completed my assessment.

> DAVID *stops pacing. Pause.*

In regards your fitness to stand trial for the murder of your wife… I'm afraid, David, but my findings at this time indicate that you suffer from anterograde amnesia, the result of which is that I'm recommending that you are unfit to stand trial. This is for your own good, David. [*Pause.*] You'll remain here until more suitable accommodation / can be—

DAVID: / Wait.

ALICE: Until more suitable accommodation can be found for you during which time your condition will be monitored for any improvement or deterioration…

DAVID: Wait.

ALICE: I'm sorry, David.

> *Pause.*

DAVID: I would like the opportunity to stand trial for the murder of my wife.

ALICE: David, please—

DAVID: And be proven guilty—

ALICE: David no—

DAVID: Wait…! Proven guilty… or otherwise… Do you believe in honour…? Do you believe in honour, Alice…? Because my wife has been murdered and this offence needs to be honoured through the criminal justice system…

> *Beat.*

ALICE: I'm sorry, David. That's a matter for the court to decide if they see fit to waive my recommendation… I sincerely hope your condition improves. [*Pause. She picks up her bag.*] Goodbye, David.

DAVID: There are two crimes here, Alice… the murder of my wife and now my continued incarceration without trial.

> *Pause.*

ALICE: David. I'm just doing my job… there's nothing I can do about it.

ALICE *moves to the door.*

DAVID: What if I am supposed to be dead? [*Pause.*] In the car… hooked up to a hose… What if I were supposed to be dead? There would be no contest. Murder-suicide. What if I'm the other victim?

DAVID *gets out the journal and flicks back through it.*

ALICE: David…?

DAVID: When was the alarm raised about the fire?

ALICE: … A neighbour, across the other side of the lake, saw the fire at 11:30. David, look—

DAVID: And the local fire authority trundled up the unsealed road to the house sometime after with their heavy vehicles and hoses… erasing all tracks. Meaning that any possibility of a third vehicle being present would be erased.

He looks in the journal.

ALICE: Goodbye, David.

DAVID: Who was she having an affair with?

ALICE: I'm so sorry.

DAVID: The fact that we were both going to be there that night was not a secret. Any number of people knew we were going to the house…

ALICE *turns to leave.* DAVID *reads from the journal.*

[*Reading*] 'Who is Reynolds?'

ALICE *stops at the door. She thinks. She turns around, sits down and opens her computer.* DAVID *watches.*

What? What are you doing?

ALICE: Wait…

She finds a file and it plays the following:

ALICE: *'You were in your office, working, doing what?'*

DAVID: *'… Finalising a brief. Why?'*

ALICE: *'Were you alone in the office?'*

DAVID: *'… No, I was with my associate. He was helping me with the brief.'*

ALICE: *'And what is his name?'*

DAVID: *'Michael Perry.'*

ALICE: *'And what else?'*
DAVID: *'... I was on the phone.'*
ALICE: *'Who to?'*
DAVID: *'My wife.'*
ALICE: *'You were on the phone to your wife ... What were you discussing?'*

> ALICE *taps on the computer.* DAVID *flicks back through the journal.*

DAVID: I don't understand…

ALICE: He was present in the room… when you called your wife.

DAVID: —

ALICE: It's not that Michael knew that you were going to be there… he knew that you weren't…

> ALICE *gathers her things and taps on the door.* DAVID *makes a note in his journal then looks up. They stare at each other.*

SCENE ELEVEN

The light in the high windows darkens. ALICE *remains by the door.* DAVID *is reading through the journal.* ALICE *puts her bag down.*

ALICE: David…? David…?
DAVID: Wait.

> *He continues to read. He flicks back a few pages, reads, and then he jumps to the last entry. He sits back in his chair and looks at* ALICE.

ALICE: David?

> DAVID *pushes the journal away and gets up and goes into the bathroom. We hear the sound of a tap running.* ALICE *slowly approaches the table. She pulls the journal toward her and turns it around. She picks it up and opens to the first page, then the second.* DAVID *comes back in wiping his face with a towel. He looks at her.*

DAVID: You read shorthand?

> *He points to the journal.*

ALICE: No.

> *She places it back on the table as* DAVID *sits on the bed.*

Do you understand what's going on, David?

DAVID *nods.*

It must be a lot to take in...

DAVID: ... Like a nightmare... a dream within a dream... [*Pause.*] Champagne... I bought a bottle of champagne. And roses... red roses...

ALICE: Yes, David. You did...

DAVID: Can I ask you something?

ALICE *sits.*

She was on the bed... wasn't she...?

ALICE: Yes, David, in the upstairs bedroom.

DAVID: Have you ever told me that?

ALICE: No... These are signs of recovery, David.

DAVID: ... I remember the rain... and the roses...

ALICE: I'm certain that with time, you'll remember everything.

DAVID: ... Why would I want to?

Pause.

ALICE: Arrangements are being made for you to be transferred to a private facility, David. But I'll continue to visit if you would like that.

DAVID *nods.*

DAVID: Has he made an admission?

ALICE: ... He says he ended the affair two weeks prior to the murder but his car was flagged at the same tollway earlier that evening. He initially lied to the police about his whereabouts but now his wife is refusing to corroborate his alibi. She's identified the gym suit as being his.

Pause.

DAVID: Why did he end it...?

ALICE: He claims he received several photographs in the mail of he and Sarah. No postmark. No message. On the back of one of the photographs was the name 'Reynolds'. He has nothing to back this up though. He says he destroyed them.

DAVID: He was being extorted?

ALICE: Lawyers make enemies, don't they, David...?

DAVID: Who is Reynolds?

ALICE: They don't know. The police believe that as a consequence of Michael ending the affair, Sarah was threatening to go public. There was a draft email buried in her personal computer, to Michael's wife, just the words 'I am having an affair with your husband'. Michael had a lot to lose... his marriage, family... his career... He is being interviewed as we speak... Perhaps, with these improvements, David, there's some hope that you'll be able to testify against him in court... Trust, betrayal and revenge.

Pause.

DAVID: How long had it been going on? The affair?

ALICE: A year... possibly more. [*Pause.*] You had the misfortune of stumbling into a murder scene. You would have pulled up at the house, seen Michael's car parked out front, gone inside... found her body in the upstairs bedroom. Michael was probably still there... in the room... waiting for you. There was an altercation... He's then dragged you downstairs and into your car. Then he found an old hose and a can of petrol in one of the outhouses... He hooked the hose up to the car... used the petrol to set fire to the house ... and then drove home to his wife and children...

DAVID: And then I've come to, disorientated and...

ALICE: Fourteen hours later you were found on the western side of the lake. [*Pause.*] He must have desperate... too many lies... threatening to unravel... and now that she was pregnant... [*Beat.*] I'm so sorry, David... I didn't mean to...

DAVID: What did you say...?

Beat.

ALICE: ... She was ten weeks pregnant at the time of her murder. [*Beat.*] ... I thought you would have known...

DAVID *goes to the table, sits and begins writing.* ALICE *watches him.*

DAVID: Do they know who...?

ALICE: The paternity...? No. It seems that she lied to you, David... about a lot of things. My sympathies... I understand... that feeling of being lied to... Well... goodbye, David.

ALICE *extends her hand but* DAVID *continues to write. After a moment she drops her hand and moves to the door and presses the buzzer. She looks back at* DAVID *writing. The door opens and she exits. The door closes and locks behind her.* DAVID *continues to write, but then stops. He gets up and takes the journal, placing it under his pillow. He then walks downstage and stares up into the CCTV camera. After a moment he turns and disappears into the bathroom. The room remains empty for a moment. The red light on the CCTV blinks away. Lights fade to black.*

SCENE TWELVE

The lights fade up to find DAVID *standing next to the bed. It's daytime. He is dressed in a shirt and suit pants and shoes. He buttons up the shirt and goes into the bathroom. When he reappears he is wearing the jacket and doing up a tie. He looks up to the high windows and pulls his watch out of his pocket, puts it on and checks the time. He raises it to his ear and listens to it ticking. The lock on the door turns and opens.* ALICE *enters carrying a computer satchel on her shoulder. The door is left open. Ambient sounds float in.*

ALICE: Hello, David… you look like a lawyer.
DAVID: Alice?

She looks at him and smiles.

ALICE: How are you?

DAVID *nods.*

DAVID: I'm good. I feel good, Alice.
ALICE: … So you'll be leaving us today?

He displays his suit.

Very nice… You're smiling… it's nice to see you smile…

DAVID *sits on the bed.*

DAVID: Thank you, Alice… I read over the journal… and I just wanted to thank you for all you have done… Couldn't have done this without you.

Beat.

ALICE: … My pleasure, David. I've come to say goodbye. You're being transferred to a private clinic, but I suspect that with these incremental improvements you won't be there for long.

Beat. DAVID *looks at his hands.*

DAVID: Incremental?

ALICE: Yes… A few days ago you asked me, 'Who is Reynolds?'… I checked back through my recordings and realised I hadn't mentioned that name since giving you the journal… So this is an island memory, David… post trauma. Given time I'm sure it will all come back…

DAVID: I'm not sure I want it to.

They stare at each other for a moment.

ALICE: So… Goodbye, David.

DAVID: Goodbye.

Beat. DAVID *extends his hand.* ALICE *moves to the bed and they shake hands.* ALICE *begins to exit but stops.*

ALICE: Oh… I have something… and I wonder if you would…

She moves to the table. She gets a book out of her bag and shows DAVID.

It's Poe. His collected works. I know you're a fan as am I… I've has this copy since I was twelve… Would you sign it for me… as a remembrance of our time together?

She slides the book across the table with a pen. DAVID *slowly moves to the table, opens the book.*

DAVID: What would you like me to write?

ALICE: 'To my biggest fan… Alice'.

DAVID *writes and slowly passes the book back.* ALICE *picks it up and looks at it.* DAVID *slowly moves back to the bed and sits.*

How wonderful… your signature… Thank you… Had a tragic life… Poe… an orphan… brutal childhood. Served in the army for a while. Dead at forty… When he died he was supposed to be travelling on his way home to New York, when he was found, delirious… wandering the streets of Baltimore. No-one knows why… He appeared to be wearing someone else's clothes. He was taken to a hospital but was never coherent enough to explain how he had found himself in this state… All he did was repeatedly call out the name 'Reynolds'.

Pause. DAVID *feels for the journal under the pillow. It's not there. At the same time* ALICE *reaches into the bag and pulls out the orange journal and places it on the table.*

… Do you know Virginia Clemm? She worked with your wife. A young intern. The police interviewed her yesterday. Asked her lots of questions about Sarah… about what she was like that day. She said that Sarah seemed normal but had been a little frustrated because she had misplaced her mobile phone… [*Pause.*] Which is odd because directly after she hung up from you at your office, a text was sent from her phone to Michael's phone with the unlisted number. To which he responded 'Yes'. [*Beat.*] Did you text him on Sarah's phone while you were still discussing the brief…?

DAVID *stands up.*

After releasing Michael at 6:00 p.m. and knowing then that he would go to the house on the lake, you waited until 8:00 p.m. and left the office. A two-hour interval… Did you change into his gym clothes in the car park or later…? You then drove there, through the rain, and just before you arrived you rang Michael, informing him that you would need him first thing Monday morning because you had decided to go to the house after all. He listened to the message and promptly left… You then arrived at the house, murdered your wife with a carving knife from the kitchen, set the upper floor on fire, rigged up the car, and wandered into the forest, to be found fourteen hours later… delirious… suffering from anterograde amnesia. Then you proceeded to leave a trail of breadcrumbs leading all the way to Michael… Means, motive, opportunity. A frame within a frame… Poe would have been proud. [*She sits at the table.*] 'I always lie'… you remember this?… Lying however is a co-operative act, isn't it, David? The power of a lie exists only in its corroboration. And that was my function. To corroborate the validity of your condition… to corroborate your affection for your wife… your genuine remorse at her loss. You needed me to be the truthseeker, stumbling blindly along the path of your 'dominant narrative'. Well, my apologies… I've always been sensitive to being 'played'.

DAVID *slowly stands up next to the bed.* ALICE *crosses and shuts the open door. He watches as* ALICE *moves back to the table.* ALICE *stares blankly at him.*

You look like you've lost something, David… Perhaps you're suffering a setback… or perhaps that mask of civility is beginning to slip…

They stare at each other.

DAVID: … Fucking bitch.

She smiles.

ALICE: … Hello, David.

Blackout. The CCTV camera blinks away.

THE END

GRIFFIN THEATRE COMPANY PRESENTS

THE HOUSE
ON THE LAKE
BY AIDAN FENNESSY

Director Kim Hardwick
Designer Stephen Curtis
Lighting Designer Martin Kinnane
Composer Kelly Ryall
Stage Manager Edwina Guinness
With Jeanette Cronin, Huw Higginson

SBW STABLES THEATRE
15 MAY - 20 JUNE

G T C
R H O
I E M
F A P
F T A
I R N
N E Y

Production Sponsor

nabprivate**wealth**   nab

Government Partners

Australian Government | Australian Council for the Arts

NSW GOVERNMENT | Trade & Investment Arts NSW

Commissioned by Black Swan State Theatre Company and
developed with the assistance of Playwriting Australia.

PLAYWRIGHT'S NOTE

My ambition when writing this play was twofold; engage an audience with an intricate narrative and to challenge myself as a writer to achieve this using only two actors and one setting. I was also keen on playing with genre. I began with a hunch about where the idea would lead but found myself in numerous cul-de-sacs during the drafting process, due to the fact that in a narrative like this, you need to mask a lot of information but not too much as you risk leaving the audience too far behind for too long.

It's also a narrative that relies as much on what is said as what is not said. Crime narrative will always, eventually, concern itself with the truth and theatre is the perfect platform in which to examine the binary oppositions of truth and lying.

The great paradox of theatre is that it is a tightly constructed lie designed to reveal truth. It's an elaborate con. The thriller used to be the real estate of theatre until film stole it in the latter part of the 20th Century. But, like any audience, the task here is to track just when, what, who, how and why.

Just as in real life, our psychic, social, emotional and sometimes physical survival depends on our ability to detect lies as well as the truth. It's been estimated that we can now expect to be lied to between 10 and 200 times on any given day. In this early part of the 21st Century you could be forgiven for thinking that lying has reached epidemic proportions. Lying is the new black. I hope you enjoy this production and thank you for supporting new Australian theatre.

Aidan Fennessy
Writer

DIRECTOR'S NOTE

I would like to write nothing about this play. No Director's Notes.

The reason for my reticence is embodied in the play itself, so with that in mind, and the knowledge that your personal experiencing of the play will follow, I'll circumvent the obstacle of Director's Notes and write 'around' the play and not 'about' it. And that statement may be in itself a clue to the nature of the material.

Persona, for Carl Jung, was the social face that the individual presented to the world, often to impress or conceal. In a theatrical context, Persona refers to the Mask.

The unmasking of both narrative and character are of particular interest and fascination in *The House on the Lake* and the consequences of that investigation isn't a state of mind that's calmed and comforted by knowledge. The revelation is chilling. A burning chill.

Theatre is a parade of personas where the tensions between what is revealed and concealed, what is true and false, what is seen or imagined, continually fascinates both the creators and the audience. The thrill of discovery never grows old.

Entrapment, ambiguity, distortion, perception, mystery, horror and the legacy of Edgar Allen Poe have been hot topics during the process of unmasking this play for the Griffin stage. It's an intriguing undertaking for a director. Where to start, what to visualise, how to resolve? A puzzle, a sturdy piece of filigree, a dark alley, a ticking bomb, a psychological minefield, a whodunit, a whydunnit?

Aidan has provided all of the above and more.

My gratitude is extended to the team at Griffin who have been uncompromising in their support of this production, however, my heart lies with the designers and cast. The stage can sometimes feel as if it's transforming into a colossal beast, devouring your value and will, but when salvation comes in the shape of collaborators of this stature then all the howling and thrashing of the creative process becomes a vocabulary that invigorates and inspires. It's a privilege to have contributed.

Kim Hardwick
Director

Aidan Fennessy
Writer

Aidan Fennessy's play *Brutopia* won the 2010 Griffin Award and his *Chilling and Killing My Annabel Lee* was part of Griffin's 1999 season. His work has also been produced by Melbourne Theatre Company, Queensland Theatre Company, HotHouse Theatre, Playbox, Rock Surfers Theatre Company and Black Swan State Theatre Company. His directing credits include, for Melbourne Theatre Company: *His Girl Friday*, *Circle Mirror Transformation*, *Return To Earth*, *Boston Marriage* and *Things We Do For Love*; for HotHouse Theatre: *The Glory* and *Oleanna*; for Playbox: *Ruby Moon*. Aidan's awards include: the Wal Cherry Award, the Barry Award, the People's Choice Award at the 2012 Premier's Literary Awards, and he has been short-listed for the Victorian Premier's Literary Award. He is the co-founder of Chameleon Theatre, and has been a member of the Artistic Directorate of HotHouse Theatre, Artistic Director of the Store Room Theatre Workshop and Associate Director at Melbourne Theatre Company.

Kim Hardwick
Director
Kim Hardwick directed the Griffin Independent production of *Unholy Ghosts* in 2014; and for Griffin Independent and The Old Fitzroy Theatre: *A Moment on the Lips*. Kim's other directing credits include, for Darlinghurst Theatre Company: *Love Song, Time Stands Still, The Memory of Water, A Day In The Death of Joe Egg* and *Dinner With Friends*; for Belvoir's B Sharp: *BANG*; and for the Seymour Centre: *The Hatpin* and *Love Bites*.

Kelly Ryall
Sound Designer
Kelly Ryall's credits for Griffin Theatre Company include: *Emerald City, The Floating World, The Boys, And No More Shall We Part, Dreams in White, Mercury Fur* and *Don't Say the Words*. His other theatre credits include, for Belvoir: *Kill The Messenger, Cinderella, Nora* and *Hedda Gabler*; for Bell Shakespeare: *As You Like It, Tartuffe, Phedre, Henry 4, Macbeth, Julius Caesar* and *The School for Wives*; for Melbourne Theatre Company: *Rupert, The Crucible, On the Production of Monsters, Return to Earth, Dead Man's Cell Phone, God of Carnage* and *Savage River*; and for Malthouse Theatre: *The Shadow King*. Kelly's compositions for dance include, for KAGE: *Flesh and Bone* and *Sundowner*; for Lucy Guerin Inc: *Pieces for Small Places*. For film, he composed for *Lois* and *One Night* and numerous television commercials. Kelly's awards include: Green Room Awards for *Love Monkey* and *Coop*, 2009; Melbourne International Arts Festival Award, 2007; Green Room Award and Fringe Festival Award for *Arabian Night*, 2005.

Stephen Curtis
Designer
Stephen Curtis' design credits for Griffin Theatre Company include: *The Floating World, Kafka Dances* and *Savage River*. His other theatre credits include, for Sydney Festival: *I Am Eora*; for West Australian Opera/Opera Queensland/ Opera Australia: *La boheme*; for Opera Australia: *Lulu and The Cunning Little Vixen*; for State Opera of South Australia: *Der Ring Des Nibelungen* (The Ring Cycle); for Sydney Theatre Company: *The Secret River, A Man With Five Children, The Government Inspector*; for Melbourne

Theatre Company: *Two Brothers* and *The Blue Room;* for Bell Shakespeare: *The Winter's Tale* and *Henry 4;* for Company B Belvoir: *Gwen in Purgatory, Small Poppies* and *Signal Driver;* for Queensland Theatre Company: *Black Diggers* and *Pygmalion.* As a production designer Stephen's film credits include *Looking for Alibrandi, Bedevil* and *Night Cries.* Stephen has recently published the book, *Staging Ideas: set and costume design for theatre as a guide to the art of theatre design.*

Martin Kinnane
Lighting Designer

Martin Kinnane's Griffin credits include: S*atango* and more recently *Unholy Ghosts* for Griffin Independent and White Box Theatre. Martin's other lighting design credits for White Box include: *The Hatpin, LoveBITES, Love Song, Who's Afraid Of Virginia Woolf?,* and *Belonging;* for Ensemble Theatre: *Six Dance Lessons In Six Weeks, End Of The Rainbow* and *Kids Stuff;* for HotHouse Theatre and Sydney Theatre Company: *Embers;* for Bell Shakespeare: *Shakespeare's R&J* and *Just Macbeth;* for Monkey Baa: *Pearlie In The Park, Sprung, Worry Worts, Emily Eyefinger* and *Fairy's Wings;* and at the Sydney Opera House: *Love Loss And What I Wore* and *Celebrity Autobiograhy.* Martin has also worked on large scale events nationally and internationally such as: World Youth Day 2008, World Masters Games 2009, and the Helpmann Awards 2006. Martin is possibly best known for his spectacularly theatrical lighting of the Sydney Harbour Bridge (the Bridge Effect) from 2000 to 2007, which has brought him international renown.

Edwina Guinness
Stage Manager

Edwina Guinness was Stage Manager for Griffin Theatre Company on *Jump for Jordan, Dreams in White* and *The Boys.* Her other theatre credits include, for Belvoir: *Blue Wizard, A Christmas Carol, Hedda Gabler, Small and Tired, Persona* and *Beautiful One Day.* Further credits as Assistant Stage Manager include, for Belvoir: *The Book of Everything, Conversation Piece, The Business, The Power of Yes;* for Sydney Theatre Company: *One Man Two Guvnors, Under Milk Wood, Bloodland, The Mysteries Genesis, Elling, War* of the Roses, Convicts Opera and Riflemind; for Malthouse Theatre: Tis Pity She's A Whore; for Bell Shakespeare: Faustus, Just Macbeth and Othello. Edwina is a graduate from VCA.

Jeanette Cronin
Alice

Jeanette Cronin's credits for Griffin Theatre Company include: The Boys, Quack, Bug and Holding the Man. Her other theatre credits include: for Sydney Theatre Company: A Doll's House, and The Crucible; for Bell Shakespeare: The Taming of the Shrew; for Belvoir: Parramatta Girls; for the State Theatre Company of South Australia: Nightletters; for Ensemble Theatre: Dark Voyager; for The Old 505 Theatre: Queen Bette and in 2014, Tell Me Again, which Jeanette wrote and performed in. Film and television credits include: Shock Room, The Boys, Terra Nova, Blackrock, Thank God He Met Lizzie, Janet King, Crownies and Rake. Jeanette was awarded the inaugural Mike Walsh Fellowship in 1996, and has received a Sydney Theatre Award Nomination for Best Supporting Actress and two nominations for the Green Room Award for Most Outstanding Actor.

Huw Higginson
David

Huw Higginson performed in the 2014 Griffin Independent show On the Shore of the Wide World. Huw's other theatre credits include, for the Bolton Octagon, UK: All My Sons, Comedians, And Did Those Feet, Demolition Man, The Winslow Boy and A Streetcar Named Desire; for Melbourne Theatre Company: Great Expectations; for Hull Truck Theatre: The Kitchen Sink; for Manchester Library Theatre: Plenty, Sergeant Musgraves Dance, Breezeblock Park. He has appeared in several television series, such as: EastEnders, Heartbeat, The Hunt, Peep Show Casualty, Doctors, Railway Murders, Secret River, Miss Fisher's Murder Mysteries, Gallipoli and Home and Away. He is best known for playing PC George Garfield in ABC/ITV's The Bill, appearing in over 600 episodes over ten years. Huw studied at The London Academy of Dramatic Art.

ABOUT GRIFFIN THEATRE COMPANY

Griffin Theatre Company is Australia's new writing theatre.

We develop and stage the best Australian stories, for the widest possible audience.

For more than 30 years, the Griffin mission has been to bring our audiences the highest standards of theatrical craft. We also have a passion for developing Australian talent, with many of our nation's most celebrated artists starting their professional careers with us.

Griffin produces an annual subscription season of four to five Main Season shows by Australian playwrights, and co-presents a season of new work with leading independent artists. We also support artists through professional development opportunities, including artist residencies and masterclasses.

Our home is the historic SBW Stables Theatre, a thriving cultural hub and Sydney's most intimate and persuasive space for actors and audiences to meet. We hope to see you here soon.

GRIFFIN THEATRE COMPANY
13 CRAIGEND ST
KINGS CROSS NSW 2011

02 9332 1052
INFO@GRIFFINTHEATRE.COM.AU
GRIFFINTHEATRE.COM.AU

SBW STABLES THEATRE
10 NIMROD ST
KINGS CROSS NSW 2011

BOOKINGS
GRIFFINTHEATRE.COM.AU
02 9361 3817

G T C
R H O
I E M
F A P
F T A
I R N
N E Y

Australian Government

Australia Council for the Arts

NSW GOVERNMENT | Trade & Investment Arts NSW

STAFF

GRIFFIN DONORS

Income from Griffin activities covers less than 40% of our operating costs – leaving an ever increasing gap for us to fill through government funding, sponsorship and the generosity of our individual supporters. Your support helps us bridge the gap, keep ticket prices affordable and our work at its best. To make a donation and a difference, contact Griffin on 9332 1052 or donate online at griffintheatre.com.au

Commission $12,500+
Anthony & Suzanne Maple-Brown
Darin Cooper Family

Studio Program
Danielle Smith
Geoff & Wendy Simpson
Gil Appleton
James Emmett & Peter Wilson
Leigh O'Neill
Limb Family Foundation
Rhonda McIver
Sophie McCarthy &
Antony Green
The Sky Foundation

Workshop $1,000-$4,999
Adrian Wiggins
Alex Byrne & Sue Hearn
Anonymous (5)
Anthony Paull
Antoinette Albert
Chris & Fran Roberts
Diana Simmonds
Dr Gae M Anderson
Dr Stephen McNamara
Ian Neuss & Penny Young
Jane Thorn
John B Fairfax AO
John Romeril
Judge Joe Harman
Larry & Tina Grumley
Libby Higgin
Luke & John Pty Ltd
Margaret Johnston
Merilyn Sleigh &
Raoul de Ferranti
Paul & Jennifer Winch
Peter Graves
Pip Rath & Wayne Lonergan
Richard & Elizabeth Longes
Richard Cottrell
Ros & Paul Espie
Russ & Rae Cottle

Reading $500-$999
Abraham Hammoud
Alex Bowen &
Catherine Sullivan
Anonymous (4)
Bill & Elaine McLaughlin
Deena Shiff &
Jim Gillespie
Henry Johnston
Isla Tooth
James Hartwright
Jan Barham
Jennifer Ledgar & Bob Lim
John Lam-Po-Tang
Jono Gavin
Judy & Sam Weiss
Karen Rodgers &
Bill Harris
Maggies Thai
Michael & Colleen
Chesterman
Michael Hobbs
Michele Lee
Natalie Pelham
Rob Macfarlan &
Nicole Abadee
Rose Hiscock
Susan Hyde
Wendy Ashton
Wendy Elder

First Draft $200-$499
Alex O Redmond
Alexandra Joel &
Philip Mason
Annie Page &
Colin Fletcher
Anonymous (4)
Aviva Ziegler
Beverley Johnson
C John Keightley
Catherine Rothery
Corinne & Bryan Everts
Danielle Hoareau
Dianne & David Russell
Duncan McKay

Elizabeth Evatt
Eric Dole
Frank Messina
Gemma Rygate
Gillian Corban
Ian & Elizabeth MacDonald
Irena Nebenzahl
Janet Heffernan
Jann Skinner
Jatesada Kongdum
Jennifer Blair
Jes Andersen
Jo Grisard
John Head
John McCallum
Julie Rosenberg
Lachlan Philpott
Leslie Jesudason
Liz Nield
Marie Delaney
Mario Philippou
Michele Dulcken
Neville Mitchell
Nicole McKenna
Nikki Barrett
Pamela Bennett
Priscilla Adey
Rebecca Rocheford Davies
Rob Brookman & Verity
Laughton
Robyn Ayres
Robyn Tantau
Ross Handsaker
Ross Kelly
Ross Steele
Sarah Miller
Shefali Rovik
Stephen Farr
Stephen Manning
Victor Cohen & Rosie McColl
Wendy Buswell
William Penhale

We would also like to thank Peter O'Connell for his expertise, guidance and time.

Current as of 30/03/2015

GRIFFIN FUND

The Griffin Fund is a new initiative focusing on education programs, leadership pathways for artists, touring Griffin productions and international exchange opportunities. Donations to the Fund are pledged for a three-year period. It is an investment in the future prospects of the company and the artists we work with. For more information please visit griffintheatre.com.au/support-us or contact our Development Manager on 9332 1052.

Founding Donors
Alison Deans & Kevin Powell
Ange Cecco & Melanie Bienemann
Annabel Ritchie
Anonymous (1)
Baly Douglas Foundation
Bruce Meagher & Greg Waters
Catherine Dovey and Kim Williams
Dr David Nguyen
Ian Phipps
Ian Robertson
John Bell & Anna Volska
Kiong Lee & Richard Funston
Lee Lewis & Brett Boardman
Lilian & Ken Horler
Lisa & Ross Lewin
Louise Walsh & Dave Jordan
Mary Holt
Michael & Charmaine Bradley
Nathan Bennet & Yael Perry
Peter & Dianne O'Connell
Peter Ingle
Simon Wellington & Sanjeev Kumar
Sophie McCarthy & Antony Green
Stuart Thomas
Will Sheehan

PRODUCTION PARTNERS

Griffin Theatre Company's Production Patrons make a direct contribution to the costs of staging a play that hasn't received corporate sponsorship. In 2015, the selected production is Angus Cerini's *The Bleeding Tree* and we are delighted to announce our inaugural supporters. For further information about the program, please contact our Development Manager on 02 9332 1052.

Bruce Meagher & Greg Waters
Carole and David Yuile
John Mitchell
Jon and Katie King
Rachel Procter
Simone Whetton
Steve Riethoff
Tina & Maurice Green

GRIFFIN SPONSORS

Griffin would like to thank the following:

Government Supporters

Australian Government | Australia Council for the Arts | NSW Government Trade & Investment Arts NSW | CREATIVE CITY SYDNEY

Patron

Seaborn, Broughton & Walford Foundation

2014 Season Sponsor

RE:

Production Sponsors

HOLDING REDLICH | nabprivatewealth nab

Foundations and Trusts

MALCOLM ROBERTSON FOUNDATION | COPYRIGHT AGENCY CULTURAL FUND | ROBERTSON FOUNDATION | GIRGENSOHN FOUNDATION

Company Lawyers

MARQUE

Dining Partner

OTTO

Company Sponsors

Time Out Sydney | THE UNIVERSITY OF SYDNEY PERFORMANCE STUDIES | Bourke Street Bakery | CURRENCY PRESS | FOUR PILLARS

MOPPITY | QUEST Potts Point Serviced Apartments | Rosenfeld, Kant & Co. Business & Financial Solutions | AVANTCard | Brett Boardman Photography | Coopers

Qbt CONSULTING | SIGNWAVE NEWTOWN | oxygen | V & R THE VICTORIA ROOM BAR RESTAURANT

Griffin Theatre Company is assisted by the Australian Government through the Australia Council, its arts funding and advisory body; and the NSW Government through Arts NSW.